MARCUS JORDAN

The life of St. Catherine of Siena

Copyright © 2024 by Marcus Jordan

All rights reserved. No part of this publication may be reproduced, stored or transmitted in any form or by any means, electronic, mechanical, photocopying, recording, scanning, or otherwise without written permission from the publisher. It is illegal to copy this book, post it to a website, or distribute it by any other means without permission.

First edition

*This book was professionally typeset on Reedsy.
Find out more at reedsy.com*

Contents

1	Introduction: Background and Early Life! Historical...	1
2	The Spiritual Journey of St. Catherine: Devotion and Early...	4
3	Theological Contributions: "The Dialogue" and Other...	8
4	Diplomacy and Church Reform: Interaction with Pope Gregory...	13
5	Catherine's Correspondence: Letters to Leaders and...	19
6	Life of Penance and Service: Commitment to Prayer and...	24
7	Canonization and Legacy: Beatification and Canonization! ...	29
8	Powerful Novena Prayer to St. Catherine of Siena	37
9	Conclusion: St. Catherine's Enduring...	46

1

Introduction: Background and Early Life! Historical Context

Background and Early Life

St. Catherine of Siena was born on March 25, 1347, in Siena, Italy, to Giacomo di Benincasa and Lapa Piagenti. The youngest of 25 children, Catherine grew up in a devout Catholic household. At an early age, she exhibited signs of exceptional piety, often withdrawing from the normal activities of childhood to focus on prayer and contemplation.

Her family, part of the lower-middle class, encouraged her to marry, but Catherine resisted, expressing a desire for a life of religious devotion. She eventually joined the Third Order of St. Dominic, committing herself to a life of poverty, chastity, and obedience.

Catherine's spiritual intensity became more apparent as she dedicated herself to a regimen of prayer, fasting, and acts of penance. It is said that she experienced mystical visions, including a spiritual marriage to Christ, which profoundly influenced her understanding of divine love.

As she grew older, Catherine's reputation for holiness spread, attracting followers and spiritual seekers. Despite lacking formal education, her profound insights into theology and spirituality gained recognition from both clergy and laity, setting the stage for her impactful role in the Catholic Church.

Historical Context

St. Catherine of Siena lived during a tumultuous period in European history marked by political strife, social upheaval, and religious challenges. The 14th century witnessed the devastating effects of the Black Death, which claimed millions of lives across the continent. Italy, where Catherine resided, faced political fragmentation with city-states vying for power.

In the midst of these challenges, the Catholic Church experienced its own turmoil. The Avignon Papacy, a period during which the papal court resided in Avignon, France, instead of Rome, raised questions about the authority and unity of the Church. Catherine's lifetime saw the Great Schism (1378–1417), a division in the Church with multiple claimants to the papal throne.

These historical circumstances greatly influenced Catherine's mission and activities. Her efforts to persuade Pope Gregory XI to return the papacy to Rome and her involvement in resolving Church conflicts were responses to the urgent need for spiritual and institutional renewal.

Against this backdrop of societal and ecclesiastical challenges, St. Catherine emerged as a charismatic figure, offering spiritual guidance and playing a crucial role in addressing the complex issues facing both the Church and society in her time.

2

The Spiritual Journey of St. Catherine: Devotion and Early Religious Experience! Mystical Visions and Spiritual Insights! The Stigmata!

Devotion and Early Religious Experiences

From an early age, St. Catherine of Siena displayed an extraordinary devotion to her faith. Drawn to a life of prayer and contemplation, she often withdrew from worldly pursuits to dedicate herself to a deepening relationship with God.

Catherine's devotion intensified as she embraced the Dominican tradition, joining the Third Order and committing to a life of poverty, chastity, and obedience. Her daily routine involved rigorous acts of penance, fasting, and long hours of prayer. This ascetic lifestyle not only reflected her personal commitment but also garnered attention from those around her.

One of the defining aspects of Catherine's spiritual journey was her experience of mystical visions. These profound encounters with the divine, including a spiritual marriage to Christ, shaped her understanding of God's love and fueled her unwavering commitment to her religious vocation.

Her mystical experiences became a source of inspiration and guidance for others seeking a deeper connection with God. Despite her lack of formal education, Catherine's spiritual insights and devotion attracted followers and established her as a revered figure within both religious and secular circles. This early phase of her life laid the foundation for the impactful role she would later play in the Church and beyond.

Mystical Visions and Spiritual Insights

St. Catherine of Siena's spiritual journey was marked by a series of profound mystical visions that deeply influenced her understanding of God and the nature of the soul. These visions, which she described in her writings, provided her with unique insights into the divine mysteries.

One notable vision was Catherine's mystical marriage to Christ, an experience in which she felt a deep union with the Savior. This encounter symbolized her profound spiritual connection and devotion to Christ, shaping her life of contemplation and prayer.

In her work, "The Dialogue," Catherine recounted dialogues with God, exploring themes of divine providence, human free will, and the transformative power of love. Through these visions, she offered profound insights into the nature of God's mercy and the importance of embracing suffering for spiritual purification.

Catherine's mystical experiences were not only personal but also had a broader impact on the communities around her. Her ability to articulate these encounters attracted followers, and her spiritual guidance resonated with individuals seeking a deeper understanding of their faith.

These mystical visions and insights became a central aspect of Catherine's spiritual legacy, contributing to her reputation as a mystic and theologian whose profound encounters with the divine continue to inspire and captivate believers centuries later.

The Stigmata

St. Catherine of Siena's profound spiritual journey reached a pinnacle with the manifestation of the stigmata, a mystical phenomenon where an individual bears the wounds of Christ on their own body. This extraordinary event occurred during one of Catherine's ecstasies, deep moments of union with God.

The stigmata in Catherine's case included the wounds corresponding to those inflicted on Christ during the crucifixion – marks on her hands, feet, and side. This physical manifestation of the Passion of Christ was not only a testament to her intense spiritual devotion but also a sign of her sharing in the suffering of Christ.

Catherine, who bore the stigmata in a hidden manner, viewed it as a divine gift and a mark of God's favor. While the stigmata was a source of great reverence among her followers, she remained humble about this extraordinary phenomenon, emphasizing the importance of inner transformation and union with God.

The occurrence of the stigmata added another layer to St. Catherine's mystical reputation, symbolizing her deep spiritual union with Christ and her willingness to embrace the physical and spiritual aspects of Christ's sacrifice. This extraordinary episode further solidified her place as a revered figure in Christian mysticism.

3

Theological Contributions: "The Dialogue" and Other Writings! Emphasis on Love and Obedience! Influence on Catholic Theology!

"The Dialogue" and Other Writings

St. Catherine of Siena's literary contributions, particularly her seminal work "The Dialogue," played a crucial role in shaping medieval Christian theology and spirituality.

"The Dialogue" (Il Dialogo della Divina Provvidenza): Completed in 1378, "The Dialogue" is a visionary and mystical work in which Catherine records her conversations with God. Divided into four parts—treatises on Divine Providence, the spiritual journey, obedience, and the role of the clergy—the text offers profound insights into the nature of God, the soul, and the transformative power of divine love. Catherine's vivid imagery and eloquent expressions make this work a masterpiece of medieval Christian literature.

Letters and Correspondence:

Despite her lack of formal education, St. Catherine wrote numerous letters to a wide range of recipients, including political leaders, clergy, and ordinary people. Her letters, marked by clarity and spiritual wisdom, addressed issues of faith, morality, and Church reform. These writings showcased her ability to navigate complex theological concepts with a direct and practical approach.

Prayers and Devotional Writings:

St. Catherine composed a collection of prayers and devotional writings that reflected her deep spirituality and intimate connection with God. These writings provided a guide for others seeking to deepen their prayer life and embrace a more profound relationship with the divine.

St. Catherine's writings not only influenced the spiritual practices of her time but continue to be studied and revered today. Her ability to articulate complex theological ideas with clarity and simplicity contributed significantly to the medieval Christian intellectual tradition.

Emphasis on Love and Obedience

Central to St. Catherine of Siena's theological teachings was an unwavering emphasis on love and obedience as essential components of the Christian life.

Love for God and Neighbor:

Catherine stressed the paramount importance of love in one's relationship with God. She believed that love was the driving force behind all virtuous actions and that a genuine love for God should naturally lead to love and compassion for one's fellow human beings. Her teachings resonated with the commandment to "love your neighbor as yourself."

The Transformative Power of Love:

Catherine viewed love as a transformative force that could purify the soul and draw individuals closer to God. She emphasized that a sincere, selfless love could overcome spiritual obstacles, fostering a deep union with the divine.

Obedience to God's Will:

In Catherine's theology, obedience was inseparable from love. She advocated for a complete surrender to God's will, aligning one's desires and actions with divine guidance. Obedience, in her view, was not a mere adherence to rules but a profound expression of love and trust in God's providence.

The Bridal Mysticism Metaphor:

Catherine frequently employed the metaphor of a spiritual marriage between the soul and God, portraying the soul as the bride and God as the divine Bridegroom. This metaphor highlighted the intimacy of the soul's union with God, grounded in love and obedience.

St. Catherine's emphasis on love and obedience continues to inspire believers, underscoring the transformative power of a deeply committed and loving relationship with the divine, as well as the importance of expressing that love through compassionate obedience to God's will.

Influence on Catholic Theology

St. Catherine of Siena's profound influence on Catholic theology is evident in several key aspects that shaped the theological landscape of her time and continue to resonate in the Church's teachings:

Mystical Theology:

Catherine's mystical experiences and writings significantly contributed to the development of mystical theology within the Catholic tradition. Her vivid descriptions of divine encounters and insights into the nature of God influenced later mystics and theologians, emphasizing the importance of a personal and experiential relationship with the divine.

Theology of Divine Love:

Catherine's emphasis on divine love as a transformative force became a cornerstone of her theological contributions. Her teachings on the transformative power of God's love, as seen in works like "The Dialogue," influenced theological perspectives on the centrality of love in the Christian life.

Papal Authority and Church Unity:

St. Catherine's involvement in the resolution of the Avignon Papacy and the Great Schism showcased her commitment to papal authority and the unity of the Church. Her efforts to persuade Pope Gregory XI to return to Rome contributed to discussions on the proper exercise of papal authority and the importance of Church unity.

Spiritual Obedience:

Catherine's teachings on obedience to God's will and the transformative nature of spiritual obedience had a lasting impact on Catholic spirituality. The integration of love and obedience as central tenets of the Christian life continues to resonate in discussions on spiritual formation and discipleship.

Theological Clarity in Vernacular Language:

Catherine, despite lacking formal education, expressed complex theological concepts with remarkable clarity in the vernacular language. This accessibility of her writings contributed to a broader dissemination of theological ideas and influenced a shift towards using the vernacular in theological discourse.

St. Catherine of Siena's influence on Catholic theology extends beyond her lifetime, as her theological insights and spiritual wisdom continue to inspire theologians, clergy, and believers seeking a deeper understanding of the Christian faith.

4

Diplomacy and Church Reform: Interaction with Pope Gregory XI! Efforts to Return the Papacy to Rome! Role in Resolving Church Conflicts!

Interaction with Pope Gregory XI

St. Catherine of Siena's interaction with Pope Gregory XI marked a pivotal moment in both her life and the history of the Catholic Church.

Plea for Church Reform:

Catherine, deeply concerned about the state of the Church, initiated correspondence with Pope Gregory XI, urging him to bring an end to the Avignon Papacy and return to Rome. Her letters emphasized the need for Church reform and the restoration of papal authority to its traditional seat.

Personal Audience with the Pope:

Catherine's reputation for holiness and spiritual insight led to a personal audience with Pope Gregory XI in Avignon. During their meeting, she passionately pleaded for the Pope to heed God's call to return to Rome, emphasizing the spiritual and moral imperative of such a move.

Success in Persuasion:

Catherine's persistence and eloquence played a significant role in influencing Pope Gregory XI's decision. In 1376, he announced his intention to return the papacy to Rome, a decision that was realized in 1377. This event marked the end of the Avignon Papacy and contributed to the restoration of the papal see to its traditional location.

Political and Spiritual Advisor:

Following the Pope's return to Rome, Catherine continued to correspond with him, offering guidance on matters of Church governance, spiritual renewal, and political affairs. Despite her lack of formal education, Catherine's insights and wisdom earned her a position as a trusted advisor to the Pope.

St. Catherine of Siena's interaction with Pope Gregory XI showcased the impact of her spiritual convictions on the highest echelons of the Church hierarchy. Her role in influencing the Pope's decision to return to Rome underscored the intersection of spiritual and political dynamics during a critical period in the history of the Catholic Church.

Efforts to Return the Papacy to Rome

St. Catherine of Siena played a pivotal role in advocating for the return of the papacy to Rome during a period known as the Avignon Papacy. Her efforts were marked by passionate appeals and diplomatic engagement:

Correspondence with Pope Gregory XI:

Catherine initiated a series of letters to Pope Gregory XI, urging him to bring an end to the Avignon Papacy and return the papal seat to Rome. In these letters, she emphasized the spiritual significance of such a move and the need for the Pope to fulfill his divine mandate.

Personal Audience in Avignon:

Catherine's reputation as a mystic and her commitment to Church reform led to a personal audience with Pope Gregory XI in Avignon. During this meeting, she fervently implored the Pope to heed God's call and emphasized the moral imperative of returning the papacy to Rome.

Spiritual Counsel and Encouragement:

Catherine provided spiritual counsel and encouragement to Pope Gregory XI, reminding him of the importance of obedience to God's will and the potential for spiritual renewal through the restoration of the papacy to its traditional seat. Her words carried weight, given her perceived holiness and connection to divine insights.

Influence on Papal Decision:

Catherine's persistent advocacy and spiritual guidance played a crucial role in influencing Pope Gregory XI's decision. In 1376, he publicly announced his intention to return the papacy to Rome, a decision realized in 1377. This move marked the end of the Avignon Papacy and the beginning of efforts to restore the papal see to Rome.

St. Catherine's involvement in the return of the papacy to Rome demonstrated the intersection of spiritual conviction and political dynamics. Her influence on Pope Gregory XI showcased the potential impact of a deeply committed individual on significant decisions within the Catholic Church.

Role in Resolving Church Conflicts

St. Catherine of Siena played a pivotal role in resolving conflicts within the Catholic Church during a turbulent period marked by the Great Schism. Her contributions to reconciliation and unity included:

Mediation Between Factions:

St. Catherine engaged in extensive correspondence with leaders and factions involved in the Great Schism, attempting to mediate and reconcile differences. She wrote letters urging unity and emphasizing the importance of putting the interests of the Church above personal or political agendas.

Appeals for Church Unity:

Catherine's letters to various ecclesiastical figures urged them to seek a resolution to the schism through dialogue and compromise. Her impassioned pleas emphasized the spiritual consequences of a divided Church and the urgency of restoring unity for the sake of the faithful.

Travel to Avignon:

In 1376, Catherine personally traveled to Avignon to meet with Pope Gregory XI and offer her counsel on resolving the schism. Her presence and persuasive abilities contributed to the Pope's decision to return to Rome, a move seen as a crucial step toward healing the divisions within the Church.

Exhortation to the Laity:

Catherine recognized the impact of laypeople in shaping the course of Church events. She encouraged the laity to remain steadfast in their faith and to support efforts for reconciliation. Her influence extended beyond the ecclesiastical hierarchy to the broader Christian community.

Emphasis on Obedience to the Papacy:

Catherine's theological teachings emphasized the importance of obedience to the Pope as a means of preserving the unity of the Church. Her stance resonated with those seeking a resolution to the schism through a reaffirmation of papal authority.

St. Catherine's active involvement in resolving Church conflicts showcased her commitment to the spiritual welfare of the Church and her belief in the power of dialogue, reconciliation, and obedience to restore unity. Her efforts left an indelible mark on the Church's history during a challenging period of division.

5

Catherine's Correspondence: Letters to Leaders and Influential Figures! Guidance on Spiritual Matters!

Letters to Leaders and Influential Figures

St. Catherine of Siena, despite her lack of formal education, demonstrated a remarkable ability to correspond with leaders and influential figures of her time. Her letters addressed various issues, combining spiritual guidance with calls for reform:

Correspondence with Pope Gregory XI:

Catherine's letters to Pope Gregory XI were instrumental in convincing him to return the papacy to Rome from Avignon. She passionately appealed to the Pope, emphasizing the urgency of the Church's need for renewal and the spiritual significance of relocating the papal seat.

Letters to Cardinals:

Catherine wrote to several cardinals, urging them to prioritize the unity of the Church and work towards resolving the Great Schism. Her letters provided spiritual insights and practical guidance on addressing the complex issues facing the Catholic Church during this turbulent period.

Appeals to Political Leaders:

Recognizing the intertwined nature of political and ecclesiastical affairs, Catherine corresponded with secular leaders, encouraging them to support efforts for Church reform and unity. Her letters addressed the importance of aligning political actions with moral and spiritual principles.

Communication with Heads of Religious Orders:

Catherine wrote to leaders of various religious orders, advocating for a return to the foundational principles of religious life. Her letters emphasized the need for spiritual renewal, adherence to vows, and a commitment to serving the Church and the greater community.

Letters to Laity and Common People:

Catherine's correspondence extended beyond the hierarchy to ordinary people. She wrote letters to individuals in various social strata, offering spiritual guidance, encouragement, and exhortations to live virtuous lives. Her letters to the laity emphasized the collective responsibility for the well-being of the Church.

In her letters, St. Catherine combined theological insights with a deep concern for the practical challenges faced by both the Church and society. Her ability to communicate effectively with a diverse audience contributed to her influence as a spiritual leader and reformer during a critical period in the history of the Catholic Church.

Guidance on Spiritual Matters

St. Catherine of Siena's guidance on spiritual matters, as conveyed through her writings and letters, encompassed a range of profound insights and practical advice:

The Primacy of Love:

Catherine consistently emphasized the centrality of love in the spiritual life. She taught that love, rooted in a deep connection with God, should be the driving force behind all thoughts, actions, and relationships.

Union with God through Prayer:

Catherine stressed the importance of prayer as a means of cultivating a close union with God. She encouraged both formal prayers and contemplative prayer, emphasizing the transformative power of communing with the divine.

Obedience to God's Will:

A recurring theme in Catherine's guidance was the significance of aligning one's will with God's. She viewed obedience to God's will not as a restrictive duty but as a path to spiritual freedom and fulfillment.

Detachment from Earthly Attachments:

Catherine advocated for detachment from material possessions and worldly ambitions. She believed that true spiritual progress required letting go of earthly attachments to focus on the eternal and the divine.

Endurance in Times of Suffering:

Catherine offered guidance on finding meaning in suffering and encouraged individuals to endure trials with patience and faith. She saw suffering not as a punishment but as a means of purification and spiritual growth.

Repentance and Reconciliation:

Catherine emphasized the importance of repentance and seeking God's forgiveness. Her guidance on the sacrament of confession and reconciliation underscored the transformative power of acknowledging one's shortcomings and seeking spiritual renewal.

Humility and Service:

Catherine placed a high value on humility, seeing it as the foundation of spiritual virtue. She encouraged a humble disposition, coupled with a commitment to serving others with love and compassion.

The Pursuit of Virtue:

Catherine's guidance centered on the cultivation of virtues such as patience, kindness, and humility. She believed that a virtuous life was essential for spiritual growth and a reflection of God's grace working within an individual.

St. Catherine's guidance on spiritual matters reflects a holistic approach, combining profound theological insights with practical advice for leading a life deeply rooted in faith, love and service.

6

Life of Penance and Service: Commitment to Prayer and Penance! Care for the Poor and Sick!

Commitment to Prayer and Penance

St. Catherine of Siena's life was characterized by a profound commitment to prayer and penance, reflecting her intense devotion to God and her understanding of the transformative power of these spiritual disciplines:

Dedication to Contemplative Prayer:

Catherine devoted significant time to contemplative prayer, seeking a deep and intimate connection with God. She believed that prayer was a means of communing with the divine and experiencing the presence of God in the depths of the soul.

Mystical Experiences in Prayer:

Catherine's commitment to prayer was accompanied by mystical experiences, including visions and a spiritual marriage to Christ. These encounters affirmed her belief in the efficacy of prayer as a channel for divine communication and transformative encounters with God.

Regular Fasting and Acts of Penance:

In addition to prayer, Catherine embraced a life of penance and self-denial. She practiced regular fasting and engaged in acts of penance as a way of expressing contrition for sins, seeking purification, and imitating Christ's sacrifice on the Cross.

Spiritual Exercises and Disciplines:

Catherine incorporated various spiritual exercises into her routine, including the Liturgy of the Hours, meditation, and reflection on sacred scripture. These disciplines were integral to her spiritual growth and played a role in shaping her theological insights.

Emphasis on Interior Conversion:

Catherine's commitment to prayer and penance was not merely external observance but aimed at fostering inner conversion. She believed that true repentance and transformation occurred at the heart level, requiring a sincere turning toward God in both thought and action.

Role Model for the Faithful:

Catherine's exemplary commitment to prayer and penance served as a model for those around her. Her followers admired her ascetic practices and sought to emulate her disciplined approach to the spiritual life.

Integration of Prayer into Daily Life:

Catherine advocated for the integration of prayer into every aspect of daily life. She saw prayer not as a separate activity but as a continuous conversation with God, permeating all actions and decisions.

St. Catherine's commitment to prayer and penance reflected her belief in the transformative power of these practices in drawing closer to God, experiencing divine grace, and cultivating a life of holiness. Her example continues to inspire individuals on their own spiritual journeys.

Care for the Poor and Sick

St. Catherine of Siena's commitment to care for the poor and sick was a central aspect of her Christian faith and lived out in practical ways:

Nursing the Afflicted:

Catherine, despite lacking formal medical training, dedicated herself to nursing the sick during times of plague. She fearlessly entered afflicted areas, providing comfort and care to those suffering, demonstrating a selfless commitment to the well-being of others.

Outreach to the Marginalized:

Catherine extended her care to the marginalized and socially excluded, recognizing the dignity of every individual. Her outreach embraced those who were often neglected by society, reflecting her belief in the inherent worth of every human being.

Establishment of a Hospice:

In Siena, Catherine established a hospice for the sick and dying. This facility became a place of solace and healing, embodying her belief in the Christian duty to serve those in need, particularly the vulnerable and suffering members of the community.

Advocacy for Social Justice:

Beyond direct care, Catherine advocated for social justice and compassion toward the less fortunate. She used her influence to speak out against injustice and inequality, challenging societal norms that perpetuated suffering and calling for a more compassionate and equitable society.

Almsgiving and Material Assistance:

Catherine encouraged almsgiving and the sharing of material resources as a way of expressing love and solidarity with the poor. Her teachings emphasized the importance of generosity and sacrificial giving to alleviate the material needs of those less fortunate.

Model of Humility:

Catherine's care for the poor and sick reflected her profound humility. Despite her own ascetic practices and mystical experiences, she humbly served those in need, seeing the face of Christ in the suffering and marginalized.

Inspiration for Social Service:

St. Catherine's example inspired later generations to engage in social service and humanitarian work. Her legacy contributed to the development of Christian charitable institutions dedicated to caring for the sick and disadvantaged.

St. Catherine's care for the poor and sick went beyond philanthropy; it was an expression of her deep understanding of Christian love in action. Her legacy continues to inspire individuals and organizations committed to serving those in need, emphasizing the importance of compassion, justice, and selfless care for the vulnerable.

7

Canonization and Legacy: Beatification and Canonization! Impact on Christian Faith! Continued Reverence and Influence!

Beatification and Canonization of St. Catherine of Siena

Beatification:

Process Initiation:

St. Catherine of Siena's journey toward beatification began shortly after her death in 1380. Recognizing her extraordinary holiness and contributions to the Church, the process was initiated to investigate her life, virtues, and the impact of her spiritual legacy.

Witness Testimonies:

Witnesses were interviewed to gather information about Catherine's life, virtues, writings, and any reported miracles associated with her intercession. The aim was to establish the heroic nature of her virtues and the impact of her sanctity on others.

Declaration of Heroic Virtues:

After a thorough examination, the Holy See declared the heroic virtues of St. Catherine of Siena. This recognition acknowledged her outstanding commitment to faith, love, and service, setting her on the path to beatification.

Beatification Decree:

The beatification decree was issued by the Pope, officially declaring St. Catherine of Siena as "Blessed." This step emphasized her exemplary life and virtue, making her worthy of veneration within the Church.

Canonization:

Miracle Investigation:

For canonization, the Church typically requires the documentation of at least one miracle attributed to the intercession of the candidate for sainthood. In St. Catherine's case, miracles would have been investigated and verified to confirm her intercessory power.

Canonization Decree:

Upon the confirmation of miracles and a thorough examination of her life and writings, the Pope issued the canonization decree, officially declaring St. Catherine of Siena a saint of the Catholic Church.

Liturgical Recognition:

Canonization involves the inclusion of the new saint in the liturgical calendar, designating a feast day for veneration by the faithful. St. Catherine's feast day is typically celebrated on April 29th.

Universal Veneration:

With canonization, St. Catherine of Siena received universal recognition as a saint, becoming a revered figure in the Catholic Church. Her life, teachings, and spiritual contributions continue to inspire believers worldwide.

The beatification and canonization of St. Catherine of Siena underscored the Church's acknowledgment of her holiness, virtuous life, and the impact of her spiritual legacy on the faithful. She is celebrated not only for her mystical experiences but also for her profound commitment to love, service, and the well-being of the Church.

Impact on Christian Faith

St. Catherine of Siena's profound impact on Christian faith is evident through various dimensions, influencing theology, spirituality, and the lives of believers:

Mystical Theology and Spirituality:

Catherine's mystical experiences and writings contributed to the development of mystical theology. Her emphasis on the intimate union with God influenced subsequent mystics and enriched the understanding of the contemplative dimension of Christian spirituality.

Ecclesiastical Influence:

Through her correspondence and efforts to resolve Church conflicts, Catherine played a role in the return of the papacy to Rome, contributing to the restoration of unity within the Catholic Church. Her influence on Pope Gregory XI showcased the potential impact of a committed individual on ecclesiastical decisions.

Devotion to Divine Love:

Catherine's teachings placed a significant emphasis on divine love as a transformative force. Her insights into the nature of God's love and the spiritual significance of love in human relationships continue to inspire Christians seeking a deeper connection with the divine.

Model of Holiness and Virtue:

Recognized for her heroic virtues, humility, and commitment to prayer and penance, St. Catherine serves as a model of holiness for Christians. Her life exemplifies the transformative power of living in accordance with Christian virtues and principles.

Legacy in Christian Literature:

"The Dialogue" and her letters continue to be studied and revered as important works in Christian literature. Her ability to articulate complex theological concepts with clarity and simplicity contributes to the intellectual and spiritual heritage of the Church.

Advocate for the Poor and Sick:

Catherine's care for the poor and sick, coupled with her advocacy for social justice, underscores the Christian call to love and serve others. Her example continues to inspire individuals and organizations engaged in charitable and humanitarian work.

Patronage and Devotion:

St. Catherine of Siena is recognized as the patron saint of Italy and the patroness of nurses and those who care for the sick. Devotion to her has spread globally, and numerous churches, institutions, and religious communities bear her name.

Influence on Christian Ethics:

Catherine's ethical teachings, rooted in love, humility, and obedience to God's will, have contributed to the ethical framework of Christian living. Her emphasis on virtue and moral principles remains relevant for Christians navigating contemporary challenges.

St. Catherine of Siena's impact on Christian faith transcends time, influencing believers across denominations and inspiring a deeper commitment to spirituality, love, and service in the name of Christ. Her legacy serves as a testament to the transformative power of faith lived out with dedication and love.

Continued Reverence and Influence

St. Catherine of Siena's influence and reverence persist through the centuries, extending far beyond her lifetime:

Spiritual Devotion:

St. Catherine remains a revered figure in Catholicism, with her feast day celebrated on April 29th. Devotees worldwide commemorate her life, seeking inspiration from her dedication to prayer, penance, and love for God.

Veneration in Art and Iconography:

Artists throughout history have depicted St. Catherine in paintings, sculptures, and other forms of art. These visual representations serve as a reminder of her spiritual legacy and continue to inspire contemplation and devotion.

Patronage and Intercession:

St. Catherine is recognized as the patron saint of Italy, nurses, and those who care for the sick. Many turn to her in prayer, seeking intercession for matters related to health, spiritual growth, and the resolution of conflicts.

Educational and Religious Institutions:

Numerous schools, churches, and religious institutions bear St. Catherine's name, reflecting the enduring impact of her teachings on education, spirituality, and Christian life.

Literary and Theological Influence:

"The Dialogue" and her letters continue to be studied by theologians and scholars. Her writings, marked by profound theological insights, serve as a source of inspiration for those exploring Christian mysticism and spirituality.

Global Devotion:

St. Catherine's influence extends beyond Catholicism, attracting a diverse range of Christians and individuals interested in spirituality. Her universal appeal highlights the timeless relevance of her teachings and example.

Continued Pilgrimage and Veneration Sites:

Pilgrims visit sites associated with St. Catherine, including her birthplace in Siena and the Basilica of San Domenico, where her head and thumb are preserved. These pilgrimage sites serve as places of reflection, prayer, and connection with her spiritual presence.

Impact on Female Spirituality:

St. Catherine is celebrated as a trailblazer for female spirituality and theological engagement. Her life challenges traditional gender roles, inspiring women to pursue a deep relationship with God and contribute actively to the Church and society.

Interfaith Appeal:

St. Catherine's teachings on love, humility, and devotion resonate with individuals of various faiths. Her inclusive message of divine love transcends denominational boundaries, fostering interfaith dialogue and understanding.

St. Catherine of Siena's continued reverence and influence affirm the enduring significance of her spiritual legacy. Her life serves as a beacon of inspiration, drawing people from diverse backgrounds to contemplate and embody the timeless virtues she espoused.

8

Powerful Novena Prayer to St. Catherine of Siena

Novena to St. Catherine of Siena - Day 1

In the name of the Father, and of the Son, and of the Holy Spirit. Amen.

O holy St. Catherine of Siena, mystic and doctor of the Church, you who, in your profound union with God, manifested an unwavering love and commitment to the Christian faith, we turn to you in this novena with gratitude and hope.

On this first day, we reflect upon your extraordinary devotion to prayer. May we, like you, find solace and strength in our communion with God. Inspire us to deepen our prayer life, seeking a closer relationship with the Divine, just as you did in your mystical experiences and intimate conversations with God.

St. Catherine, you understood the transformative power of

prayer; intercede for us, that our prayers may draw us nearer to God and lead us on the path of holiness.

(Pray the Our Father, Hail Mary, and Glory Be.)

St. Catherine of Siena, pray for us. Amen.

Novena to St. Catherine of Siena – Day 2

In the name of the Father, and of the Son, and of the Holy Spirit. Amen.

O holy St. Catherine of Siena, you who exemplified heroic virtues, particularly humility, we continue our novena seeking your intercession.

On this second day, we reflect upon your profound humility and selflessness. Your life was marked by a genuine acknowledgment of your dependence on God and a humble service to others.

St. Catherine, help us cultivate true humility in our hearts. May we learn to recognize our weaknesses, seeking God's mercy and grace. Inspire us to serve others with selfless love, as you did, putting their needs before our own.

(Pray the Our Father, Hail Mary, and Glory Be.)

St. Catherine of Siena, model of humility, pray for us. Amen.

Novena to St. Catherine of Siena - Day 3

In the name of the Father, and of the Son, and of the Holy Spirit. Amen.

O holy St. Catherine of Siena, mystic and peacemaker, we continue our novena seeking your intercession.

On this third day, we reflect upon your role in promoting unity within the Church. Your efforts to resolve conflicts and restore the papacy to Rome exemplify your commitment to the Church's well-being and the importance of unity among believers.

St. Catherine, intercede for us, that we may contribute to the unity of the Church and foster harmony among fellow Christians. May our actions and words be guided by a desire for peace and reconciliation.

(Pray the Our Father, Hail Mary, and Glory Be.)

St. Catherine of Siena, peacemaker of the Church, pray for us. Amen.

Novena to St. Catherine of Siena - Day 4

In the name of the Father, and of the Son, and of the Holy Spirit. Amen.

O holy St. Catherine of Siena, who devoted yourself to a life of prayer and penance, we turn to you on this fourth day of our novena.

Reflecting on your commitment to prayer and penance, we seek your intercession. Help us deepen our prayer life, surrendering our will to God's, just as you did. Inspire us to embrace penance as a means of purification and drawing closer to the Divine.

St. Catherine, guide us on the path of spiritual discipline, that our lives may reflect the transformative power of a heart devoted to God.

(Pray the Our Father, Hail Mary, and Glory Be.)

St. Catherine of Siena, example of prayer and penance, pray for us. Amen.

Novena to St. Catherine of Siena – Day 5

In the name of the Father, and of the Son, and of the Holy Spirit. Amen.

O holy St. Catherine of Siena, who dedicated yourself to the care of the poor and sick, we approach you on this fifth day of our novena.

Reflecting on your compassionate service to those in need, we seek your intercession. Inspire us to emulate your love for the marginalized, the sick, and the vulnerable. May we recognize the face of Christ in those who suffer and respond with selfless acts of kindness and mercy.

St. Catherine, intercede for us, that our hearts may be open to the needs of others, and our hands ready to serve as instruments of God's love.

(Pray the Our Father, Hail Mary, and Glory Be.)

St. Catherine of Siena, patroness of the sick and compassionate servant, pray for us. Amen.

Novena to St. Catherine of Siena - Day 6

In the name of the Father, and of the Son, and of the Holy Spirit. Amen.

O holy St. Catherine of Siena, whose life exemplified a profound love for God and an unwavering commitment to obedience, we turn to you on this sixth day of our novena.

Reflecting on your emphasis on obedience to God's will, we seek your intercession. Help us surrender our desires and plans to the divine guidance of the Lord. May we find true freedom in aligning our will with His, just as you did in your life of devoted obedience.

St. Catherine, guide us on the path of humble submission, that our lives may be a testament to the transformative power of trusting in God's providence.

(Pray the Our Father, Hail Mary, and Glory Be.)

St. Catherine of Siena, model of obedience, pray for us. Amen.

Novena to St. Catherine of Siena - Day 7

In the name of the Father, and of the Son, and of the Holy Spirit. Amen.

O holy St. Catherine of Siena, mystic and teacher of divine love, we approach you on this seventh day of our novena.

Reflecting on your writings, especially "The Dialogue" and your profound insights into the transformative power of divine love, we seek your intercession. Help us to understand, embrace, and share the boundless love of God in our lives. May our hearts be filled with the same fervor and passion for God's love that characterized your spiritual journey.

St. Catherine, intercede for us, that we may be vessels of divine love in a world that longs for the healing and transformative touch of God's grace.

(Pray the Our Father, Hail Mary, and Glory Be.)

St. Catherine of Siena, mystic and teacher of divine love, pray for us. Amen.

Novena to St. Catherine of Siena - Day 8

In the name of the Father, and of the Son, and of the Holy Spirit.

Amen.

O holy St. Catherine of Siena, who played a vital role in the resolution of Church conflicts and the restoration of unity, we turn to you on this eighth day of our novena.

Reflecting on your efforts for Church unity, we seek your intercession. Inspire in us a commitment to fostering harmony and understanding within the Body of Christ. May we actively work towards the unity of all believers, recognizing our shared faith in Christ.

St. Catherine, intercede for us, that we may be instruments of reconciliation and builders of unity within the Church and in our relationships with others.

(Pray the Our Father, Hail Mary, and Glory Be.)

St. Catherine of Siena, champion of Church unity, pray for us. Amen.

Novena to St. Catherine of Siena - Day 9

In the name of the Father, and of the Son, and of the Holy Spirit. Amen.

O holy St. Catherine of Siena, whose life was a testament to the transformative power of faith, we come to you on this ninth and final day of our novena.

As we conclude this novena, we reflect on the impact of your devotion, teachings, and unwavering faith. We seek your intercession for our spiritual journey. May we, like you, be anchored in a deep and authentic relationship with God, drawing strength from our faith to face life's challenges.

St. Catherine, guide us in our continued pursuit of holiness, and intercede for us in our spiritual endeavors.

(Pray the Our Father, Hail Mary, and Glory Be.)

St. Catherine of Siena, mystic and beacon of faith, pray for us. Amen.

Final Novena Prayer to St. Catherine of Siena

O holy St. Catherine of Siena, mystic, teacher, and exemplar of Christian virtue, we conclude this novena with hearts filled with gratitude for your intercession.

Through these nine days, you have guided us in reflecting on your life, virtues, and unwavering commitment to God. We thank you for your example of deep prayer, humility, obedience, and compassionate service to the poor and sick.

As we conclude this novena, we entrust our intentions to your care. May your prayers strengthen our faith, deepen our love for God, and inspire us to live lives of holiness and service.

St. Catherine, patroness and friend, continue to intercede for us before the throne of grace. Pray for our needs, both known and unknown, and assist us on our journey toward God.

We ask this through Christ our Lord. Amen.

9

Conclusion: St. Catherine's Enduring Significance! Reflection on her Spiritual Legacy!

St. Catherine's Enduring Significance

St. Catherine of Siena's enduring significance is marked by her profound impact on spirituality, theology, and the Christian life. Her legacy persists through the following dimensions:

Mystical Theology:

St. Catherine's mystical experiences and writings, notably "The Dialogue," contribute to the rich tapestry of Christian mysticism. Her teachings on the soul's journey towards union with God continue to inspire seekers of deeper spiritual understanding.

Theological Influence:

Recognized as a Doctor of the Church, St. Catherine's theological insights have left an indelible mark. Her ability to articulate complex theological concepts with clarity and simplicity remains a valuable resource for theologians and scholars.

Model of Holiness:

St. Catherine's virtuous life, marked by prayer, humility, obedience, and compassionate service, serves as a model of holiness. She continues to inspire believers to cultivate these virtues in their own lives, fostering a deeper relationship with God.

Peacemaker and Church Reformer:

St. Catherine's role as a peacemaker during the Great Schism and her efforts in influencing the return of the papacy to Rome showcase her impact on Church history. Her commitment to unity within the Church remains relevant, encouraging dialogue and reconciliation.

Patronage and Devotion:

St. Catherine is recognized as the patroness of Italy, nurses, and those who care for the sick. Devotion to her spans the globe, with numerous churches, institutions, and religious communities bearing her name.

Literary Contribution:

St. Catherine's writings, letters, and "The Dialogue" continue to be studied and admired for their eloquence and depth. Her literary contributions remain a source of inspiration for those exploring Christian spirituality and theology.

Female Spirituality and Leadership:

St. Catherine's life challenges traditional gender roles, making her a trailblazer for female spirituality and leadership within the Church. She stands as a beacon for women seeking to actively contribute to the Church and society.

Global Devotion and Pilgrimage:

Pilgrims from around the world visit sites associated with St. Catherine, underscoring her global appeal. Pilgrimage to her birthplace in Siena and other locations connects believers with her spiritual presence.

St. Catherine of Siena's enduring significance lies in her timeless teachings, virtuous example, and the transformative power of her faith. Her influence continues to shape the spiritual landscape, resonating with individuals seeking a deeper understanding of God and a more meaningful Christian life.

Reflection on St. Catherine of Siena's Spiritual Legacy

St. Catherine of Siena, a beacon of spiritual light in the medieval Church, leaves behind a profound legacy that resonates across centuries. Her life and teachings invite reflection on several key aspects of her spiritual legacy:

Passionate Love for God:

St. Catherine's legacy begins with her intense love for God. Her writings, filled with poetic expressions of divine love, invite us to consider the depth of our own love for the Creator. In a world often marked by distractions, Catherine's unwavering passion for God challenges us to rekindle the flames of our spiritual ardor.

Contemplative Prayer:

At the heart of St. Catherine's spirituality is contemplative prayer. Her mystical experiences and dialogues with God inspire us to delve deeper into our prayer lives. She reminds us that prayer is not merely a routine but an intimate conversation with the Divine, a pathway to encounter the profound mysteries of God's love.

Humility and Obedience:

St. Catherine's life exemplifies humility and obedience to God's will. Her unwavering submission to divine guidance, even in the face of challenges, prompts us to reflect on our own willingness to surrender to God's plan. In a world that often celebrates self-sufficiency, Catherine teaches us the transformative power of humble obedience.

Advocacy for Unity:

St. Catherine's efforts to reconcile the Church during the Great Schism underscore her commitment to unity. Her legacy challenges us to be peacemakers in our communities, promoting harmony and understanding. She invites us to consider how we contribute to the unity of the Church and the broader human family.

Compassionate Service:

St. Catherine's care for the poor and sick reveals a compassionate heart. Her legacy prompts us to reflect on our own commitment to serving those in need. She teaches us that true spirituality involves active love and practical assistance to those who suffer, embodying the Christian call to be Christ's hands and feet in the world.

Writing as a Spiritual Tool:

St. Catherine's prolific writings, including "The Dialogue" and her letters, serve as spiritual tools that continue to guide believers. Her legacy encourages us to explore the transformative power of writing in our own spiritual journeys, whether through journaling, letters, or other forms of expression.

Trailblazer for Women in Faith:

As a Doctor of the Church and a woman who actively engaged in theological and ecclesiastical matters, St. Catherine challenges traditional gender roles. Her legacy calls for a reflection on the role of women in the Church and society, inspiring a more inclusive and equitable approach.

St. Catherine of Siena's spiritual legacy is a timeless invitation to embark on a journey of love, prayer, humility, and service. As we reflect on her life, we are prompted to examine our own spiritual landscapes, seeking ways to deepen our relationship with God and live out the transformative principles she so passionately embraced. Her legacy endures as a guiding light, urging us to draw closer to the divine and to live lives of profound love and service.

Printed in Great Britain
by Amazon